Fitness + Health Fundamentals

A Resource Guide for Active Living

Sixth Edition

Allison Nye
Cape Fear Community College

Kendall Hunt
publishing company

Pages 7-12, 13, and 69: From Fitness & Your Health, 2nd edition by David Nieman. Copyright © 2005 by Kendall Hunt Publishing Company. Reprinted by permission.

Figures 3.1-3.4, page 16; figure 3.5, page 21; figures 3.6-3.8, pages 22-23; and table 3.1, page 22; From Fitness & Your Health, 2nd edition by David Nieman. Copyright © 2005 by Kendall Hunt Publishing Company. Reprinted by permission.

Cover image © Shutterstock, Inc.

www.kendallhunt.com
Send all inquiries to:
4050 Westmark Drive
Dubuque, IA 52004-1840

Copyright © 2006, 2009, 2011, 2013, 2016, 2019 by Allison Nye

ISBN 978-1-5249-8821-0

CONTENTS

Chapter 1: Course and Lab Manual Outline Introduction 1

    Purposes of the Course and Lab Manual 1
    Lab Manual Objectives 1
    Gym Approval Form 2

Chapter 2: Understanding and Self-Assessing Health, Wellness, and Fitness 3

    Five Components of Health 3
    Six Components of Skill 3
    Personal Feelings about Physical Fitness and Health 4
    Fitness and Wellness Questionnaire 5
    Living Long and Healthfully: A Self-Test 7
    What Does Your Score Mean? 12

Chapter 3: Preparing for Physical Activity 13
        Are You Ready to Exercise?

    Physical Activity Readiness Questionnaire (PAR Q) 13
    Fitness Assessments 14
    Physical Fitness Assessment Record Form 15
    Extra Credit for PED 110 Students taking an On-Campus Class 17
    Measuring Your Heart Rate 18
    Determining Your Target Heart Rate 19
    Karvonen Formula Chart 21
    Perceived Exertion Rating Scale 22
    Perception of Exertion Assignment 23
    Body Composition Assessment 25

Chapter 4: Achieving Goals and Behavior Change 27

    S.M.A.R.T.—Specific, Measureable, Action, Realistic, Time-Oriented 27
    Goal Setting Checklist 29
    Behavior Change Contract 31
    Stages of Lifestyle Change 31

Chapter 5: Weekly Tracking and Recording 33

    Cardiovascular Training Log (2) 51

    Physical Activity Record (2) 55

    Resistance Training Log 59

    Resistance Training Record 61

    Designing and Implementing a Progressive Fitness Plan 63

Chapter 6: Workouts 67

    Dynamic Warm-Up Exercises 69

    Cardiovascular/Muscular Strength/Endurance and Flexibility Workout 71

    Bodyweight Exercises 73

    Bodyweight Circuit and Bodyweight Exercises for Interval Training 74

    Level 1.1 77

    Level 1.2 78

    Level 1.3 79

    Level 1.4 80

    Level 2.1 81

    Level 2.2 82

    Level 2.3 83

    Level 2.4 84

    Level 2.5 85

    Level 3.1 86

    Level 3.2 87

    Upper body circuit 1 88

    upper body circuit 2 89

    Quick Lower body circuit 90

    HIIT random 91

    The Name Game workout 92

    Design Your Own Workout 93

Chapter 7: Mindfulness and Relaxation Labs 95

    Meditation Intro 97

    Progressive 4-Week Yoga Program 98

Course and Lab Manual Introduction

Being physically fit and healthy is a journey and a lifelong pursuit that does not have to be elusive. Everyone can achieve some level of physical fitness. This course is designed to either start you on your journey of a healthy lifestyle or meet you wherever you may be in your current fitness program. Fitness is dynamic and always changing. Fitness is not something you capture and then you have it. Once you attain a level of fitness you are comfortable with, you must continue to work to maintain that current level. Whether you are new to exercise or have been training for years, this class and lab manual will provide resources to accomplish growth or help you choose the training path that best suits you and your circumstances. So, let's get started! We hope you enjoy the journey.

Physical fitness is not only one of the most important keys to a healthy body;
it is the basis of dynamic and creative intellectual activity.
—John F. Kennedy

PURPOSE OF THE COURSE AND LAB MANUAL

This course is designed to investigate and apply the basic concepts and principles of lifetime physical fitness and other health-related factors. Lab emphasis is placed on optimal wellness through the application of fitness, exercise, and healthy lifestyle concepts.

LAB MANUAL OBJECTIVES

1. Identify healthy lifestyles.

2. Describe the components of fitness and health.

3. Describe the benefits of physical activity and healthy lifestyles.

4. Determine what it means to be physically fit.

5. Design a personalized fitness program based on appropriate needs and goals.

6. Apply guidelines for safe and effective exercise.

GYM APPROVAL FORM

A GYM MEMBERSHIP IS REQUIRED for online PED students

*A workout facility at an apartment complex is not approved. See the full list of pre-approved gyms located in Blackboard.

Please fill out the following and upload to your instructor in the Document Sharing section during week 1 of class.

1. **Facility name, address, and phone number-**

2. **Facility Contact Person** (preferably a gym manager)- Find a gym representative and list their name.

3. **Permission to access your records-** YES/NO. If NO, you will not be able to receive any Gym Lab credit.

4. Your short-term and long-term fitness **GOALS** for the semester. Be specific and detailed.

Short-term-

Long-term-

5. Verify by **signing below** you have spoken to a gym representative regarding the gym being able to provide a printout of ALL of your login records from your scanned membership card. The gym must be able to provide a copy of your electronic card swipe records, or you will lose 15% of your overall Gym Lab grade (see syllabus).

Sign the following statement:

"I _____have spoken to gym employee_____
and they have confirmed that at the end of this course, the gym will supply a printout of my electronic login records for every card swipe each time I entered and exited the gym. And I am aware if I do not submit a printout of my gym login/logout records at the end of the course, I will receive a zero for 15% of my overall grade."

SIGN YOUR NAME AND DATE_____date_____

Options on how to upload and submit the Gym Approval Form:

Option 1) Scan the signed Gym Approval Form and upload. Use a phone app to scan if needed.

Option 2) Recreate/type the signed Gym Approval Form form as a WORD/PDF document and upload.

Source: Allison Nye

2

Understanding and Self-Assessing Health, Wellness, and Fitness

On a scale of 1 to 5, rate your level of fitness based on the eleven health and skill-related components.

FIVE COMPONENTS OF HEALTH

1. Cardiovascular   _____

2. Muscular Strength   _____

3. Muscular Endurance   _____

4. Flexibility   _____

5. Body Composition   _____

SIX COMPONENTS OF SKILL

1. Agility   _____

2. Balance   _____

3. Coordination   _____

4. Power   _____

5. Speed   _____

6. Reaction Time   _____

What does it mean to be physically fit and healthy to you?

What does being physically active mean to you? What elements are most important for you? How would you describe your past experiences in Physical Education? As a child what activities do you remember doing? Based on your past physical education, fitness, and health experiences, describe below in two paragraphs or more how you feel about being physically active and what it means to you.

_____

_____

_____

_____

_____

_____

_____

_____

_____

_____

_____

_____

_____

_____

_____

_____

Name _____   Date _____

Fitness and Wellness Questionnaire

Answer the following questions:

1. Are you currently involved in a fitness program? If so, which activities?

    _____

    _____

    _____

2. What components of fitness are these activities classified as? Cardiovascular?

    _____

    _____

    _____

3. If you are not currently involved in a fitness program, describe why not. Also, which activities would you like to begin?

    _____

    _____

    _____

4. There is always room for improvement. What areas would you like to improve if you already have a fitness program established?

    _____

    _____

    _____

5. Do you consider your position at work to be sedentary, moderately active, or active?

_____

6. List some of your hobbies or interests, other than exercise.

_____

_____

_____

7. How would you best describe your personality?

____Competitive and motivated

____Easy going and relaxed

____Quiet and reserved

8. How many hours of sleep do you get at night? _____

9. Do you have any personal goals related to fitness? If so, please elaborate.

_____

_____

_____

_____

10. Are you a member of a gym? If so, what gym are you a member of? Are you satisfied with the facilities and services provided?

_____

_____

_____

Living Long and Healthfully: A Self-Test

A long, high quality life is not a gift but rather the reward of wise lifestyle choices. While some people may live long because this "runs in the family," the vitality, fitness, and health they enjoy during the final years of their lives is heavily dependent on personal health habits.

This self-test will help you understand just how closely you adhere to a wide variety of recommended health practices. The choices you make now to improve your personal health habits will have much to do with the quality of the rest of your life.

Directions: Circle one number at the far right of each category that best represents your personal lifestyle. When finished, total all the numbers circled, and apply the result to the norms listed at the end.

1. Cigarette Smoking

A.	Never smoked or quit more than 15 years ago	0
B.	Ex-smoker, quit 5 to 15 years ago	3
C.	Ex-smoker, quit within last 5 years	5
D.	Current smoker, less than 20 cigarettes per day	9
E.	Current smoker, 20 to 40 cigarettes per day	12
F.	Current smoker, more than 40 cigarettes per day	15

2. Beverage Consumption (Alcohol, Coffee, Water)

Alcohol: How many alcoholic drinks do you consume? (A standard alcoholic drink contains .5 oz. of ethanol, which is found in a 12 fl. oz. can of beer, a 4.5 fl. oz. glass of wine, or one ounce of 100 proof distilled spirits or whiskey).

A.	Never use alcohol	0
B.	Less than once per week	2
C.	1 to 6 times per week	5
D.	Once per day	7
E.	2 to 3 per day	9
F.	More than 3 per day	13

Coffee: How many cups (6 fl. oz.) of coffee (do not include decaffeinated) do you drink?

A.	Never use coffee	0
B.	Less than once per week	1
C.	1 to 6 times per week	2
D.	Once per day	3
E.	2 to 4 per day	4
F.	More than 4 per day	6

Water: How many glasses (8 fl. oz.) of water do you drink per day?

A.	More than 6 glasses per day	0
B.	4 to 6 glasses per day	1
C.	Less than 3 per day	4

3. Diet

Note: Carefully note the portion sizes as you answer the questions. In addition, remember to include amounts used in cooking and mixed dishes.

Fruits and vegetables (l/2 to 1 cup)

5 or more servings each day	0
2 to 4 servings each day	2
1 or less servings each day	3

Grain products (breads, cereals, pasta, rice) 1 slice/1/2 cup

6 or more servings each day	0
3 to 5 servings each day	2
2 or less servings each day	3

Red meats (beef, pork, lamb, veal; not fish or poultry) 3 oz.

Seldom or never use	0
Less than once per week	2
1 to 4 per week	3
5 to 6 per week	5
Daily	7

Cheeses (do not include cottage or low fat cheese), 1 oz.

Seldom or never use	0
Less than once per day	1
More than once per day	2

Whole milk (not low fat/skim), 1 cup

Seldom or never use	0
Less than once per day	1
More than once per day	2

Eggs (including yolk) 1 whole

Seldom or never use	0
1 or 2 per week	1
3 or 4 per week	2
More than 4 per week	3

4. Exercise/Fitness

Outside of your normal work or daily responsibilities, how often do you engage in exercise that moderately increases your breathing and heart rate, and makes you sweat, for at least 20 continuous minutes, such as in brisk walking, cycling, swimming, jogging, aerobic dance, etc.?

A.	5 or more times per week	0
B.	3 to 4 times per week	1
C.	1 to 2 times per week	3
D.	Less than 1 time per week	5
E.	Seldom or never	7

5. Desirable Weight

How would you rate your body weight?

A.	Very close to ideal	0
B.	About 10% too high	2
C.	About 11 to 25% too high	5
D.	About 26 to 40% too high	7
E.	More than 40% too high	10

6. Mental/Social/Spiritual Wellbeing

A. In general, how satisfied are you with your life?

Mostly satisfied	0
Partly satisfied	1
Mostly disappointed	3

B. How often do you get insufficient rest so that you are unable to function efficiently?

Less than weekly	0
Usually one night per week	1
2 or 3 nights per week	2
4 or more nights per week	3

C. How would you describe the emotional stress you experience:
On the job (which includes being a student):

Experience average or low levels of stress	0
Experience much stress but am able to cope with it	1
Experience much stress and often feel unable to cope	3

At home:

Experience average or low levels of stress	0
Experience much stress but am able to cope with it	1
Experience much stress and often feel unable to cope	3

D. Have you suffered a serious personal loss or misfortune in the past year? (For example, divorce, separation, jail term, death of a close person, job loss, disability)?

No	0
Yes, one serious loss	2
Yes, two or more serious losses	4

E. How many friends and relatives (including your spouse) do you feel close to? (People that you feel at ease with, can talk to about private matters, and can call on for help).

10 or more	0
5 to 9	1
1 to 4	2
None	3

F. How would you describe your spiritual health?

Good to Excellent	0
Fair to Poor	2
Very Poor	4

"Optimal spiritual health is defined as the ability to develop one's spiritual nature to its fullest potential. This includes our ability: to discover, articulate and act on our own basic purpose in life; to learn how to give and receive love, joy and peace; to pursue a fulfilling life; and to contribute to the improvement of the spiritual health of others."

[*Am J Health Promotion* 1(2):12–17, 1987.]

7. Personal Factors

A. Among your close relatives (parents, grandparents, aunts, uncles), how many deaths from heart disease or cancer have occurred before age 60?

None	0
1	2
2 or more	5

B. What percent of the time do you use seat belts while driving or riding?

100 %	0
50–99 %	2
25–49 %	4
Less than 25% of the time	6

C. How often do you see your physician for a physical check up?

At least once per year	0
Only once every three years	2
Only once every last five years	4

D. Your blood pressure is:

Low or normal (less than 120/80 mm Hg)	0
Borderline high (120/80 to 139/89)	3
Moderately high (140/90 to 159/94)	8
Very high (160/95 and higher)	12

E. Your serum cholesterol is:

Low (less than 180 mg/dl)	0
Borderline high (180–199 mg/dl)	3
Moderately high (200–239 mg/dl)	8
Very high (240 mg/dl and higher)	12

*If you do not know your blood pressure, we highly recommend that you get it measured very soon. To complete the self-scoring test, you can estimate your blood pressure ranking by evaluating two lifestyle factors: body weight and salt intake. If your body weight and sodium intake are optimal, your risk of high blood pressure is greatly lowered.

**If you do not know your serum cholesterol, we highly recommend that you get it measured very soon. To complete the self-scoring test, you can estimate your serum cholesterol ranking by evaluating several lifestyle factors: saturated fat, dietary cholesterol, and dietary fiber intakes, body weight, and regular exercise. If your dietary intake of meats and dairy products (which are high in saturated fat and cholesterol) is low, while your intake of whole grains, fruits, and vegetables (rich in dietary fiber) is high, and your body weight and physical activity levels are at desirable levels, there is a good chance your serum cholesterol level is low.

What Does Your Score Mean?

Score	Rating	Explanation
0 to 20	Excellent	Congratulations! You adhere very well to the recommended lifestyle. Your potential for increased longevity and decreased risk of both heart disease and cancer are very high.
21 to 40	Very Good	If you find yourself in this category, you are probably only one or two lifestyle habits away from earning an excellent rating. You've already made wonderful progress—keep up the good work.
41 to 70	Fair	Many Americans will find themselves in this category. To fall in this category, you may not have but one or two outstanding health problems. However, due to several less than optimal health practices in a wide variety of areas, your point total has reached an undesirable level. By gradually working on selected areas, improving health practices that you are presently motivated to act on, you can steadily progress to the "excellent" rating. Improved longevity and quality of life will be your reward.
71 to 95	Poor	Your risk of heart disease, cancer, and early death is high. Now is the time to sit down with your spouse or close friends and establish health behavior change goals, following the principles outlined in this book. There are many case histories of people who have turned their health lifestyles completely around, reaping abundant health benefits. The human body responds fruitfully to an improved lifestyle, often repairing some of the damage already experienced.
96 to 140	Very Poor	Unusually high risk of early death due to heart disease and/or cancer. You are urged to make an appointment with your physician to have a thorough check up, and to seek counseling for an improved lifestyle.

3

Preparing for Physical Activity Are You Ready to Exercise?

PHYSICAL ACTIVITY READINESS QUESTIONNAIRE (PAR Q)

Regular physical activity is fun and healthy, and increasingly more people are starting to become more active every day. Being more active is very safe for most people. However, some people should check with their doctor before they start becoming much more physically active.

Fitness Assessments

Cardiovascular

1. One Mile Walk Test—used to assess those with low to moderate aerobic fitness levels

2. Three Minute Step Test—used to assess moderate to high aerobic fitness levels

3. Twelve Minute Run Test—used to assess moderate to high aerobic fitness levels

4. One Mile Jog Test—used to assess those with moderate to high aerobic fitness levels

5. One and One-Half Mile Run Test—used to assess those with moderate to high aerobic fitness levels

Muscular Strength and Endurance

1. Push-Ups—used to assess upper body including triceps, anterior deltoid, and pectoralis muscles

2. Curl-Ups—used to assess abdominal muscle strength and endurance

Flexibility

1. Sit and Reach—used to assess flexibility of hamstrings

Body Composition

1. Hip to Waist Ratio—

2. Body Fat Analysis—

3. Body Mass Index (BMI)—

4. Height-Weight Measurement—

5. Frame Size Measurement—

Skill-Related Fitness

1. Vertical Jump Test—

2. Agility Run—

3. Three-Second Speed Test—

Name _____   Age_____

Physical Fitness Assessment Record Form

	date/score	date/score	date/score	date/score
1. Curl-Ups (1 minute)				
2. Push-Ups (1 minute)				
3. Sit and Reach				
4. One-Mile Walk Exercise Heart Rate (EHR)				
5. Step Test (3 minutes) (EHR)				
6. 12 Minute Run (EHR) 1 Mile Run 1.5 Mile Run (EHR)				
7. Body Fat %				
8. Body Mass Index (BMI)				

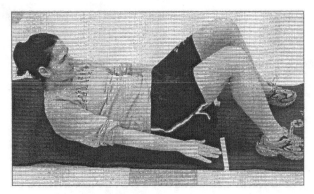

Figure 3.1
Curl-up test

Figure 3.2
Push-up test for males and females

Figure 3.3
The 1-RM bench press test

Figure 3.4
The sit-and-reach flexibility test

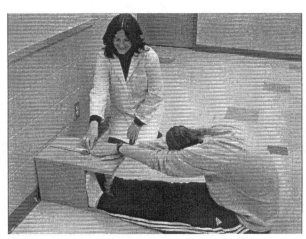

If you meet the following criteria you will have the opportunity to gain one (1) point on your final grade for EACH fitness assessment completed. A total of three (3) points may be added to your grade at the end of the semester. Each fitness assessment will be administered by your instructor.

- **1 Mile Run: 8 minutes or less**

  Pre test score-

  Post test score-

- **Push Ups in 1 minute: Men- 50   Women- 45**

  Pre test score-

  Post test score-

- **Sit and Reach: Men- 21 inches   Women- 22 inches**

  Pre test score-

  Post test score-

Activity 1: Measuring Your Heart Rate

1. Use your fingertips, not your thumb, to find your pulse at your carotid or radial artery.

2. Count the number of times your heart beats for 10 seconds.

3. Multiply the number of times your heart beats by 6 to get your heart rate in beats per minute (bpm).

4. Other methods include:
    A. Count the number of beats for 15 seconds and multiply by 4.
    B. Count the number of beats for 30 seconds and multiply by 2.

Resting Heart-Rate Measurements

10 seconds x 6 =_____bpm

15 seconds x 4 =_____bpm

30 seconds x 2 =_____bpm

First morning: _____bpm

Second morning   _____bpm

Third morning   _____bpm

Average   _____**bpm**

DETERMINING YOUR TARGET HEART RATE

Calculation of Target Heart Rate

1. **Maximal Heart Rate** (maxHR) = 208 — (.7 x age)

    The formula is useful for all activity levels and both genders.

2. **Percent of Heart Rate Reserve Method** (HRR)

    Max heart rate minus resting heart rate = heart rate reserve (HRR)

    To calculate **threshold:**

    HRR x 40% (.40) + resting heart rate

    To calculate **upper limit/high end:**

    HRR x 85% (.85) + resting heart rate

3. **Percent of Maximal Heart Rate**

    To calculate **threshold:**

    Maximal heart rate x 55% (.55)

    To calculate **upper limit/high end:**

    Maximal heart rate x 85% (.85)

TRAINING HEART RATE ZONE
USING THE KARVONEN FORMULA

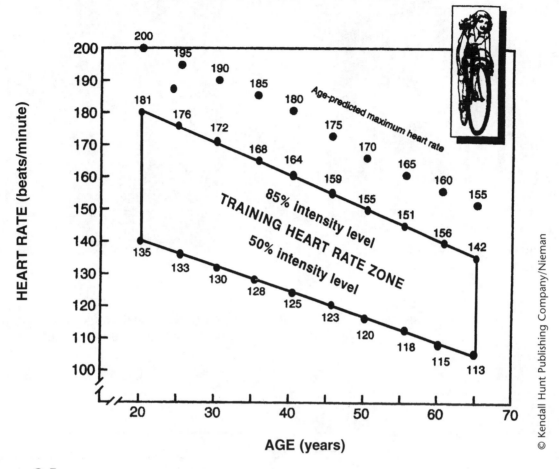

Figure 3.5

Maximal heart rates and the training heart rate zone for people of varying ages using the Karvonen formula. The resting heart rate is assumed to be 70 bpm.

Relatively few Americans get regular, planned exercise which is basic to fitness in advanced societies. The ordinary tasks of daily living no longer provide enough vigorous exercise to develop and maintain good muscle tone or cardiovascular and respiratory fitness.

—President's Council on Physical Fitness

Image © 2008. Used under license from Shutterstock, Inc.

Figure 3.6
To measure the training heart rate during exercise, the participant should stop periodically and count his pulse, using the carotid pulse.

Figure 3.7
Heart rates can be accurately monitored using chest-strap transmitters that wirelessly signal the heart rate to a monitor on the wrist.

Table 3.1 Perceived Exertion Rating Scale

	Light Intensity	
	6	No exertion at all
	7	Extremely light
	8	
	9	Very light
	10	
	11	Light

	Moderate Intensity	
	12	
	13	Somewhat hard
	14	

	Vigorous Intensity	
	15	Hard (heavy)
	16	
	17	Very hard
	18	
	19	Extremely hard
	20	Maximal exertion

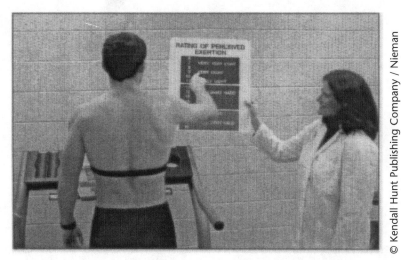

Figure 3.8
The RPE scale is a good indicator of exercise intensity.

PERCEPTION OF EXERTION ASSIGNMENT

Rate your perception of exertion during physical activity. This feeling should reflect how intense and strenuous the exercise feels to you. All feelings and sensations of effort, fatigue, and physical stress should be considered. Try to focus on your overall feeling.

Look at the rating scale while you are engaging in an activity. Choose the number (6–20) that best describes your exertion level. Appraise your feeling of exertion.

BODY COMPOSITION ASSESSMENT

1. Use the scale to determine/record your body weight.

    - Weight _____lbs.

    - Height in inches _____

2. Calculate and record your percent body fat and BMI and using the **bioelectrical impedance body fat analyzer**. Use your textbook for recommendations/ratings.

    - Percent body fat- _____

    - Body fat rating- _____

    - BMI- _____

    - BMI rating- _____

    Fitness Goals:

4

Achieving Goals and Behavior Change

In order for your goals to be meaningful, you must follow certain criteria. When formulating goals and evaluating success, your goals should be written using the following guidelines. Goals must be *specific*. Stating that you would like to lose weight, gain weight, add bulk, or run faster is not sufficient. Rather, state how much weight you want to lose or gain, or how fast you want to be able to run, etc. Your goals must also be *attainable*. It would be great if we could all be in the Olympics, but for the majority of us it is not something attainable. How do you know if you have met your goal? You must decide on a clear way to *measure* the outcome of your efforts. You should be able to say, "Yes, I have definitely met my objective," or you need to rethink your plan.

S.M.A.R.T.

SPECIFIC

MEASUREABLE

ACTION, REALISTIC, TIME-ORIENTED

When it is obvious that the goals cannot be reached,
don't adjust the goals, adjust the action steps.
—Confucius

27

GOAL SETTING CHECKLIST

1. Why do you want to begin an exercise program or why are you currently exercising?

2. What motivates you?

3. What activities do you enjoy?

4. Do the activities you are currently doing provide fun and enjoyment?

5. How often do you commit to exercise?

6. How do you feel during exercise?

7. What are your outcome goals?

8. What are your specific goals?

9. Do you think you can schedule and organize your day to make exercise happen? How?

BEHAVIOR CHANGE CONTRACT

Please complete the following:

I, _____ would like to _____ _____

by (include a date) _____.

Currently, I (describe your current level)_____.

Plan of attack for accomplishing my goal:

_____

_____

_____

_____

Goal Reevaluation:

_____

_____

_____

_____

We are what we repeatedly do.
Excellence, then, is not an act, but a habit.
—Aristotle

STAGES OF LIFESTYLE CHANGE

How Motivated for Change Are You?

Maintenance:	I regularly practice healthy lifestyles.
Action:	I have made some lifestyle changes.
Preparation:	I am getting ready to make a lifestyle change.
Contemplation:	I am thinking about change.
Precontemplation:	I don't want to change.

5

Weekly Tracking and Recording

Never discourage anyone...who continually makes progress, no matter how slow.
—Plato 427 BC–347 BC

(c) Billionspics/Shutterstock.comç

Weekly Plan #1: _____ to _____

CARDIO			
ACTIVITY	LEVEL	DISTANCE	MINUTES

WEIGHTS			
ACTIVITY	WEIGHT	REPS	SETS
Shoulders			
Chest			
Back			
Triceps			
Biceps			
Quads			
Hamstrings			
Calves			
Abs			

GOAL TRACKER			
ORIGINAL	CURRENT	CHANGE	AMOUNT REMAINING

Weekly Plan #2: _____ to _____

CARDIO			
ACTIVITY	LEVEL	DISTANCE	MINUTES

WEIGHTS			
ACTIVITY	WEIGHT	REPS	SETS
Shoulders			
Chest			
Back			
Triceps			
Biceps			
Quads			
Hamstrings			
Calves			
Abs			

GOAL TRACKER			
ORIGINAL	CURRENT	CHANGE	AMOUNT REMAINING

Weekly Plan #3: _____ to _____

CARDIO			
ACTIVITY	LEVEL	DISTANCE	MINUTES

WEIGHTS			
ACTIVITY	WEIGHT	REPS	SETS
Shoulders			
Chest			
Back			
Triceps			
Biceps			
Quads			
Hamstrings			
Calves			
Abs			

GOAL TRACKER			
ORIGINAL	CURRENT	CHANGE	AMOUNT REMAINING

Weekly Plan #4: _____ to _____

CARDIO			
ACTIVITY	LEVEL	DISTANCE	MINUTES

WEIGHTS			
ACTIVITY	WEIGHT	REPS	SETS
Shoulders			
Chest			
Back			
Triceps			
Biceps			
Quads			
Hamstrings			
Calves			
Abs			

GOAL TRACKER			
ORIGINAL	CURRENT	CHANGE	AMOUNT REMAINING

Weekly Plan #5: _____ to _____

CARDIO			
ACTIVITY	LEVEL	DISTANCE	MINUTES

WEIGHTS			
ACTIVITY	WEIGHT	REPS	SETS
Shoulders			
Chest			
Back			
Triceps			
Biceps			
Quads			
Hamstrings			
Calves			
Abs			

GOAL TRACKER			
ORIGINAL	CURRENT	CHANGE	AMOUNT REMAINING

Weekly Plan #6: _____ to _____

CARDIO			
ACTIVITY	LEVEL	DISTANCE	MINUTES

WEIGHTS			
ACTIVITY	WEIGHT	REPS	SETS
Shoulders			
Chest			
Back			
Triceps			
Biceps			
Quads			
Hamstrings			
Calves			
Abs			

GOAL TRACKER			
ORIGINAL	CURRENT	CHANGE	AMOUNT REMAINING

Weekly Plan #7: _____ to _____

CARDIO			
ACTIVITY	LEVEL	DISTANCE	MINUTES

WEIGHTS			
ACTIVITY	WEIGHT	REPS	SETS
Shoulders			
Chest			
Back			
Triceps			
Biceps			
Quads			
Hamstrings			
Calves			
Abs			

GOAL TRACKER			
ORIGINAL	CURRENT	CHANGE	AMOUNT REMAINING

Weekly Plan #8: _____ to _____

CARDIO			
ACTIVITY	LEVEL	DISTANCE	MINUTES

WEIGHTS			
ACTIVITY	WEIGHT	REPS	SETS
Shoulders			
Chest			
Back			
Triceps			
Biceps			
Quads			
Hamstrings			
Calves			
Abs			

GOAL TRACKER			
ORIGINAL	CURRENT	CHANGE	AMOUNT REMAINING

Weekly Plan #9: _____ to _____

CARDIO			
ACTIVITY	LEVEL	DISTANCE	MINUTES

WEIGHTS			
ACTIVITY	WEIGHT	REPS	SETS
Shoulders			
Chest			
Back			
Triceps			
Biceps			
Quads			
Hamstrings			
Calves			
Abs			

GOAL TRACKER			
ORIGINAL	CURRENT	CHANGE	AMOUNT REMAINING

Weekly Plan #10: _____ to _____

CARDIO			
ACTIVITY	LEVEL	DISTANCE	MINUTES

WEIGHTS			
ACTIVITY	WEIGHT	REPS	SETS
Shoulders			
Chest			
Back			
Triceps			
Biceps			
Quads			
Hamstrings			
Calves			
Abs			

GOAL TRACKER			
ORIGINAL	CURRENT	CHANGE	AMOUNT REMAINING

Weekly Plan #11: _____ to _____

CARDIO			
ACTIVITY	LEVEL	DISTANCE	MINUTES

WEIGHTS			
ACTIVITY	WEIGHT	REPS	SETS
Shoulders			
Chest			
Back			
Triceps			
Biceps			
Quads			
Hamstrings			
Calves			
Abs			

GOAL TRACKER			
ORIGINAL	CURRENT	CHANGE	AMOUNT REMAINING

Weekly Plan #12: _____ to _____

CARDIO			
ACTIVITY	LEVEL	DISTANCE	MINUTES

WEIGHTS			
ACTIVITY	WEIGHT	REPS	SETS
Shoulders			
Chest			
Back			
Triceps			
Biceps			
Quads			
Hamstrings			
Calves			
Abs			

GOAL TRACKER			
ORIGINAL	CURRENT	CHANGE	AMOUNT REMAINING

Weekly Plan #13: _____ to _____

CARDIO			
ACTIVITY	LEVEL	DISTANCE	MINUTES

WEIGHTS			
ACTIVITY	WEIGHT	REPS	SETS
Shoulders			
Chest			
Back			
Triceps			
Biceps			
Quads			
Hamstrings			
Calves			
Abs			

GOAL TRACKER			
ORIGINAL	CURRENT	CHANGE	AMOUNT REMAINING

Weekly Plan #14: _____ to _____

CARDIO			
ACTIVITY	LEVEL	DISTANCE	MINUTES

WEIGHTS			
ACTIVITY	WEIGHT	REPS	SETS
Shoulders			
Chest			
Back			
Triceps			
Biceps			
Quads			
Hamstrings			
Calves			
Abs			

GOAL TRACKER			
ORIGINAL	CURRENT	CHANGE	AMOUNT REMAINING

CARDIO			
ACTIVITY	LEVEL	DISTANCE	MINUTES

WEIGHTS			
ACTIVITY	WEIGHT	REPS	SETS
Shoulders			
Chest			
Back			
Triceps			
Biceps			
Quads			
Hamstrings			
Calves			
Abs			

GOAL TRACKER			
ORIGINAL	CURRENT	CHANGE	AMOUNT REMAINING

Weekly Plan #16: _____ to _____

CARDIO			
ACTIVITY	LEVEL	DISTANCE	MINUTES

WEIGHTS			
ACTIVITY	WEIGHT	REPS	SETS
Shoulders			
Chest			
Back			
Triceps			
Biceps			
Quads			
Hamstrings			
Calves			
Abs			

GOAL TRACKER			
ORIGINAL	CURRENT	CHANGE	AMOUNT REMAINING

Name _____   Age _____   Start Date _____

Cardiovascular Training Log

Exercise	Date	Duration	Intensity	Scale from 6–20 Perceived Exertion	# of Laps

The sovereign invigorator of the body is exercise,
and of all the exercises walking is the best.
—Thomas Jefferson

Name _____   Age _____   Start Date _____

Cardiovascular Training Log

Exercise	Date	Duration	Intensity	Scale from 6–20 Perceived Exertion	# of Laps

The sovereign invigorator of the body is exercise,
and of all the exercises walking is the best.
—Thomas Jefferson

Name _____   Section # _____

Physical Activity Record

Record your workout on the specific activity log in addition to the log below:

Date/Time	Type of Activity	Duration (Min)	Intensity (RPE)	Verified

Name _____ Section # _____

Physical Activity Record

Record your workout on the specific activity log in addition to the log below:

Date/Time	Type of Activity	Duration (Min)	Intensity (RPE)	Verified

Name _____   Age _____   Weight _____

Resistance Training Log

Exercise	Date	Wt/Reps	Wt/Reps	Wt/Reps

Resistance Training Record

Section # _____

Name _____

Procedure: Fill in the appropriate date, weight, and repetitions used during each exercise session.

Exercise		Chest		Back		Legs		Biceps/Triceps		Abdominals	
Date	Lbs.										
	Reps										
Date	Lbs.										
	Reps										
Date	Lbs.										
	Reps										
Date	Lbs.										
	Reps										
Date	Lbs.										
	Reps										
Date	Lbs.										
	Reps										
Date	Lbs.										
	Reps										
Date	Lbs.										
	Reps										
Date	Lbs.										
	Reps										
Date	Lbs.										
	Reps										

Designing and Implementing a Progressive Fitness Plan

The chart below should be used to represent a 1 week fitness plan. Each week apply the 10% rule of progression in order to achieve benefits. Do greater amounts of each activity weekly by implementing the overload principle and increasing the frequency, intensity, and time.

Type of Exercise	Exercise	Time	Intensity	Reps/Sets weight
Warm-up				
Cardio				
Muscular Endurance and Strength				
Cool-Down				
Flexibility				

	Saturday				
	Friday				
	Thursday				
	Wednesday				
	Tuesday				
	Monday				
	Sunday				

Workouts

If it Doesn't Challenge You, it Won't Change You

© Undrey/Shutterstock.com

Dynamic Warm-Up Exercises

- The purpose of a warm-up is to gradually get your heart rate up, to prevent injury, and to prepare your body for your main workout. The warm-up is the first phase of a workout and should be performed for 5 to 15 minutes.

Sample Warm-up Exercises:

- High Knee Walk

- Walking Lunges

- Frankenstein Walk

- Bodyweight Squats

- Mountain Climbers

- Leg Swings

- Sideways Jumping Jacks

- Walk on Heels

- Back Pedal

CARDIOVASCULAR/MUSCULAR STRENGTH/ENDURANCE AND FLEXIBILITY WORKOUT

Complete the following exercises in 20 minutes in no particular order:

1. **Lunges:** 3 sets of 15x

2. **Push-ups:** 3 sets x 30 or more

3. **Jumping Jacks:** 3 sets x 40

4. **Squats:** 3 sets x 12

5. **Curl-ups or Crunches:** 3 sets x 25

Complete the following in 20 minutes:

6. **Cardiovascular Activity:** 20 minutes of a team sport or walk/jog (**HR up to 150 BPM**)

Complete the following flexibility exercises in 10 minutes or more:

7. From the flexibility chapter in your textbook, perform ten major group **stretches** (2 sets @ 15 seconds)

© ostill/Shutterstock.com

Bodyweight Exercises

- Perform all body weight exercises slowly and under control to get the best results and avoid injury. Go through each of these exercises 3 times, take minimal amounts of rest in between each exercise and then take 1-2 minutes in between each series of exercises.

- The key to this workout is progression. You should push for more reps each time. Apply the 10% rule weekly.

Arms-

- Pull-Ups

- Dips

- Push-ups

- Decline Push-ups

- Diamond Push-ups

Trunk-

- Plank

- Side Plank

- Crunch

- Reverse Crunch

- Dorsal Raise

- Superman

- Burpee

Legs-

- Squat, Jump Squat

- Lunges

- Wall Sit

- Single Leg Mini Squat

- Bridge

- Heel Drops

- 50 Squats
- 10 Squat jumps
- 20 Pushups
- 20 Lunges (10 on each side)
- Hold the plank for 60 seconds
- 50 Jumping jacks
- 30 Mountain climbers
- 20 Crunches
- 20 Abdominal cycles

- Burpee × 10 reps
- Rest 60 seconds and Repeat 3–8 times
- Burpee with 2 push ups × 10 reps
- High knees × 50 reps
- Repeat 3–8 times
- Burpee × 30 seconds
- High knees × 30 seconds
- Rest 30 seconds
- Squats or jump squats × 30 seconds
- Fast mountain climber × 30 seconds
- Rest 90 seconds and repeat full circuit 2–3 times

- High knees × 20 seconds
- Rest 10 seconds and repeat 3–8 times
- High knees × 100 reps
- Rest 60 seconds and repeat 3–8 times
- Push ups × 10, 9, 8, etc.
- High Knees × 30 seconds
- Countdown, 10 push ups then high knees, 9 push ups high knees, etc.

- Squat or jump squats—20 seconds
- Hold in bottom squat position—10 seconds
- Repeat 5–8 times
- Squat or jump squat—20, 18, 16, 14, 12, 10 reps
- Fast mountain climbers—20 seconds
- Countdown, squat 20, fast mountain climbers, squat 18, fast mountain climbers, etc.
- Squat or jump squat × 20 reps

- High knees × 20 reps
- Repeat 5 times as quickly as possible
- Fast mountain climbers × 20 seconds
- Rest 10 seconds and repeat 4–8 times
- Fast mountain climbers × 30 seconds
- Front plank × 30 seconds
- Repeat 3–8 times
- Fast mountain climbers × 30 seconds
- Squats × 30 seconds
- Rest 30 seconds and repeat 3–8 times

Level 1:

Introductory HIIT Routine

Total Time: 9:00

Repeat the set three (3) times. Rest for one (1) minutes after each set.

	<u>WORK</u>	<u>REST</u>
SPRINT	0:20	0:10
SQUAT	0:20	0:10
JUMPING JACK	0:20	0:10
PUSH-UP	0:20	0:10

Source: Allison Nye

HITT LEVEL 1

TOTAL TIME: 10:00

Repeat the set two times. Rest one minute after each set.

	WORK	REST
SPRINT	0:30	0:00
SQUAT	0:30	0:00
SEAL JACK	0:30	0:00
PUSH-UP	0:30	0:00
HIGH KNEES	0:30	0:00
REVERSE LUNGE	0:30	0:00
THE MUMMY	0:30	0:00
PLANK	0:30	0:00

HITT LEVEL 1

TOTAL TIME: 12:00

Complete all three rounds in order. Rest one minute after each round.

	Round 1 WORK/REST	Round 2 WORK/REST	Round 3 WORK/REST
JUMPING JACK	0:15/0:15	0:20/0:10	0:30/0:00
LATERAL LUNGE	0:15/0:15	0:20/0:10	0:30/0:00
MOUNTAIN CLIMBER	0:15/0:15	0:20/0:10	0:30/0:00
X-JACK	0:15/0:15	0:20/0:10	0:30/0:00
SQUAT HOLD	0:15/0:15	0:20/0:10	0:30/0:00
PUSH-UP	0:15/0:15	0:20/0:10	0:30/0:00

HITT LEVEL 1

TOTAL TIME: 27:00

Complete each set three times. Rest for one minute after each set.

	WORK/REST	WORK/REST
SET 1		
HIGH KNEES	0:30	0:0
SEAL JACK	0:30	0:0
SPRINT	0:30	0:0
CROSS JACK	0:30	0:0
SET 2		
SQUAT	0:30	0:0
REVERSE LUNGE	0:30	0:0
SQUAT LIFT (RIGHT)	0:30	0:0
SQUAT LIFT (LEFT)	0:30	0:0
SET 3		
THE MUMMY	0:30	0:0
PUSH-UP	0:30	0:0
PLANK	0:30	0:0
BICYCLE CRUNCH	0:30	0:0

HIIT Level 2

Total Time: 8:00

Repeat the set two (2) times. Rest for 30 seconds after each set.

	WORK	REST
SKATER JUMP	0:20	0:30
SQUAT	0:20	0:30
BURPEE	0:20	0:30
MOGUL JUMP	0:20	0:30
SQUAT JUMP	0:20	0:30
1-2 PUSH	0:20	0:30

HIIT Level 2

Intro

Total Time: 9:00

Repeat the set three (3) times. Rest for one (1) minutes after each set.

	WORK	REST
CROSS-COUNTRY SEAL	0:30	0:00
BURPEE	0:30	0:00
SKI SQUAT	0:30	0:00
TIGER PUSH-UP	0:30	0:00

HITT LEVEL 2

TOTAL TIME: 10:00

Repeat the set two times. Rest one minute after each set.

	WORK	REST
SPRINT	0:30	0:15
SKATER JUMP	0:30	0:15
SQUAT PEDAL	0:30	0:15
1-2 PUSH	0:30	0:15
LATERAL LUNGE	0:30	0:15
CROSS PUSH	0:30	0:15
SPRINTER SIT-UP	0:30	0:15
PLANK	0:30	0:15

HITT LEVEL 2

TOTAL TIME: 22:30

Complete each set three times. Rest for 30 seconds after each set.

	WORK/REST	WORK/REST
SET 1		
JUMPING JACK	0:30	0:0
SQUAT JUMP	0:30	0:0
SPRINT	0:30	0:0
JUMP LUNGE	0:30	0:0
SET 2		
BURPEE	0:30	0:0
T-STAND (RIGHT)	0:30	0:0
SKATER JUMP	0:30	0:0
T-STAND (LEFT)	0:30	0:0
SET 3		
V-UP	0:30	0:0
1-2 PUSH	0:30	0:0
PLANK PUNCH	0:30	0:0
SPRINTER SIT-UP	0:30	0:0

HITT LEVEL 2

Complete each set two (2) times. Rest for 30 seconds after each set.

	WORK/REST	WORK/REST
SET 1		
SPRINT	0:30	0:0
GRASSHOPPER	0:30	0:0
X-JACK	0:30	0:0
MOUNTAIN CLIMBER	0:30	0:0
SET 2		
SQUAT	0:30	0:0
REVERSE LUNGE	0:30	0:0
SQUAT JUMP	0:30	0:0
JUMP LUNGE	0:30	0:0

HITT LEVEL 3

TOTAL TIME: 15:00

Repeat the set three times. Rest one minute after each set.

	WORK	REST
SPRINT	0:30	0:00
JUMP LUNGE	0:30	0:00
GRASSHOPPER	0:30	0:00
STAR	0:30	0:00
BALL PRESS	0:30	0:00
SQUAT JUMP	0:30	0:00
BURPEE	0:30	0:00
PLANK ROTATION	0:30	0:00

HITT LEVEL 3

TOTAL TIME: 15:00

Repeat the set three times. Rest one minute after each set.

	WORK	REST
X- JACK	0:30	0:00
1-2 PUSH	0:30	0:00
REACH	0:30	0:00
STAR	0:30	0:00
SKI SQUAT	0:30	0:00
TIGER PUSH-UP	0:30	0:00
CRAB TOUCH	0:30	0:00
IN-AND-OUT ABS	0:30	0:00

Upper-Body Workout: Circuit 1

Repeat Circuit 3x

1. Overhead Press
8-12 reps
Hold a set of dumbbells and create 90-degree angles with each arm so upper arms are parallel to the ground and dumbbells are at about head height. As you exhale, press the weights overhead (without clanking the weights together). Return to the starting position, not letting elbows drop below shoulder height to keep some resistance.

2. Triceps Kickback
8-12 reps
Hinge forward from your hips, keeping core tight and flat back. Bending elbows, glue your upper arms to your sides. On an exhale, straighten your arms as much as possible. Inhale to bend elbows back to starting position. Be sure to maintain a neutral spine and neck position.

3. Chest Press
8-12 reps
Lie face-up on a mat. Bring elbows out in line with shoulders to create a 90-degree angle. Press the weights up without clanking them together, focusing on engaging the muscles in your chest. Lower weights back to the starting position.

Upper-Body Workout: Circuit 2

Repeat Circuit 3x

1. Side Plank with Lateral Raise
8-12 reps per side

Start in a side plank (either full or modified by keeping your bottom knee on the floor) and hold a light dumbbell in your top hand. Bring weight in front of the center of your core. Keeping your arm slightly bent, lift weight up to shoulder height. Return to starting position. For even more of a challenge, you can lift your top leg and touch it to the weight between each rep.

2. Push-Up
15 reps

Start in plank position with hands planted directly under shoulders (slightly wider than shoulder-width apart). Ground your toes into the floor to stabilize the bottom half of your body. Keeping your spine straight (don't lift hips, and keep neck in line with your spine instead of dropping it forward) and knuckles pressing into the floor, lower your body until your chest almost grazes the floor. Exhale as you press back up.

3. Triceps Dip
8-12 reps

Slowly lower your body as you inhale by bending at the elbows until you lower yourself far enough to where there is an angle slightly smaller than 90 degrees between the upper arm and the forearm. Tip: Keep the elbows as close as possible throughout the movement. Forearms should always be pointing down.

Quick Lower Body Circuit

1. BULGARIAN SPLIT SQUATS 10x per side

2. SQUATS 20x

3. GLUTE BRIDGES 30x

4. SPRINTER SIT-UPS 40 per side

5. JUMPING JACKS 1 MINUTE

6. REST 1 MINUTE

REPEAT 3x

Exercise	Repetitions	Notes
Squat Press	20 Total	Modified: Drop the weights when form falters.
Push-up Row	20 Total	Modified Exercise: Perform push-ups from knees.
Mountain Climbers	20 Each Leg	Modified Exercise: Perform high knees in place.
Lunge With Curl	20 Total	Modified Exercise Perform squat curl.
Plank Front Raise	20 Total	Modified exercise: Remove the front raise and perform exercise on knees.
Burpees With Push-up	20 Total	Modified exercise: Remove the push-up; walk down to bottom position and walk back up.

Bonus Exercise: Finish with 6 x 200 meter sprints.

The Name Game Workout

A = 50 Jumping Jacks

B = 20 Crunches

C = 30 Squats

D = 15 Push-ups

E = 1 min Wall Sit

F = 10 Burpees

G = 15 Mountain Climbers

H = 20 Squats

I = 30 Jumping Jacks

J = 15 Crunches

K = 10 Push-ups

L = 2 min Wall Sit

M = 20 Burpees

N = 10 Burpees

O = 40 Jumping Jacks

P = 15 Mountain Climbers

Q = 30 Crunches

R = 15 Push-ups

S = 30 Burpees

T = 15 Squats

U = 15 Mountain Climbers

V = 3 min Wall Sit

W = 20 Burpees

X = 60 Jumping Jacks

Y = 10 Crunches

Z = 20 Push-ups

DESIGN YOUR OWN

WORKOUT

1. Must include all major muscles groups- list muscles used for each exercise
2. Must include planks- record time and sets
3. Must include push-ups- record how many
4. Must include a warm-up and a cool-down- name exercises and stretches
5. Must include reps/sets/lbs/time if applicable
6. Must include heart rate at the peak of the workout

- WARM-UP (light cardio)

  _____
  _____
  _____

- MAIN WORKOUT- CHOOSE 10 EXERCISES

  _____
  _____
  _____
  _____
  _____

- Heart rate after 10 minutes _____bpm

- Heart rate after 20 minutes _____bpm

- COOL-DOWN (can include stretches, yoga, or Pilates)

  _____
  _____
  _____
  _____
  _____
  _____
  _____
  _____

7

Mindfulness and Relaxation Labs

Happiness is when what you think, what you say, and what you do are in harmony.

—Mahatma Gandhi

CHANGE STARTS IN THE MIND

Meditation Intro

Meditation can be a useful and important form of stress management, creating a sense of introspection and personal renewal. There are many different forms of meditation. Most forms of meditation involve sitting quietly for 15 minutes or longer.

Find a quiet place where you can do your meditation practice. Once you have found your quite space, see if you can allow yourself 5 minutes. Revisit the practice and increase your time.

STEP 1: Take your seat

STEP 2: Find your sitting posture

STEP 3: Notice and follow your breath

STEP 4: Note the thoughts and feelings that arise

STEP 5: Nice work! You've successfully completed your first meditation experience.

Progressive 4-Week Yoga Program

Yoga is a practice that incorporates relaxation, stretching, and breathing movements. The goal is to bring a greater balance to body and mind.

MATERIALS NEEDED: Choose a mat that will provide traction.

LOCATION: Choose a space that is quite and calm. Yoga can be practiced anywhere large enough to lay down a mat.

CLOTHING: Clothing that is comfortable and allows for movement is recommended.

GOAL: Practice a basic yoga sequence two to four times a week. Slowly progress to 120 minutes a week by week four. Each session should be 30 to 60 minutes.

Order of poses:

Corpse

Cat/Cow

Spinal Balance

Downward Facing Dog

Warrior 1

Triangle

Downward Facing Dog

Warrior 2 Cat/Cow

Extended Angle

Corpse

Downward Facing Dog

Warrior 1

Triangle

Warrior 2

Extended Angle